OUR WORLD WORKBOOK LEVEL 2

NATIONAL GEOGRAPHIC

SERIES EDITORS

Joan Kang Shin

JoAnn (Jodi) Crandall

AUTHOR

Jill Florent

NATIONAL GEOGRAPHIC LEARNING | CENGAGE Learning

Australia • Brazil • Japan • Korea • Mexico • Singapore • Spain • United Kingdom • United States

Unit 0

1 **Listen and look.** Write. Use words from the box. TR: 02

> aunt   cousin   dad   grandma   grandpa
> me   mom   sister   uncle

My Family

2 **Read and look.** Write the number.

1. Close your book.
2. Go to the board.
3. Take out your crayons.
4. Hold up your card.
5. Be quiet!

6. Open your book.
7. Work in a group.
8. Raise your hand.
9. Work with a partner.

❸ Listen and write. Use words from the box. TR: 03

I	our
he	she
her	their
his	they
it	we
its	you
my	your

1.

2.

1. _____ is eating _____ sandwich.

   _____ is eating _____ apple.

2. _____ have _____ crayons.

   _____ have _____ books.

3. _____ am wearing _____ hat.

   _____ are wearing _____ hat.

4. What is the dog wearing?

   _____ is wearing _____ jacket.

3.

4.

❹ Listen and find. Circle TR: 04

3

Unit 1

Fun in Class

1 **Look and write.**

counting	cutting	gluing	listening	reading
writing	coloring	drawing	erasing	talking

He's _____.

He's _____.

He's _____.

She's _____.

She's _____.

He's _____.

4

She's _____

She's _____.

She's _____.

He's _____.

2 **Work with a partner.**

Point. Ask and answer.

Who is reading?

He's reading.

5

3 **What are we doing?** Look. Write. Use words
from the box.

reading   writing   talking   listening
counting   gluing   cutting   drawing

1. We're _____.

   We're _____.

   We're coloring pictures.

2. We're _____.

   We're _____.

   We're _____ to

   our teacher.

4 **Listen.** Check your answers to Activity 3. TR: 05

5 **Think.** Draw. Write.

What are you doing today? What are you doing in your classroom?

We're _____.

6

GRAMMAR

What **are** you doing?   We**'re erasing** the board. | **we're** = we + are

6 **Look.** Draw yourself in the pictures.
What are you doing? Write.

We're cutting.

We_____.

We_____.

We_____.

7

7 **Look and listen.** Write numbers. TR: 06

 ☐

 ☐

 ☐

 ☐

8 **Listen again.** Write sentences. TR: 07

1. _____   3. _____

2. _____   4. _____

9 **Look.** Answer the question. Write a sentence.

> coloring   cooking   counting   cutting
> eating   reading   watching TV

What are you doing?   What are you doing?   What are you doing?

1. We're _____   2. _____   3. _____

10 **Match.** Draw lines.

glue

a marker

a notebook

a paintbrush

scissors

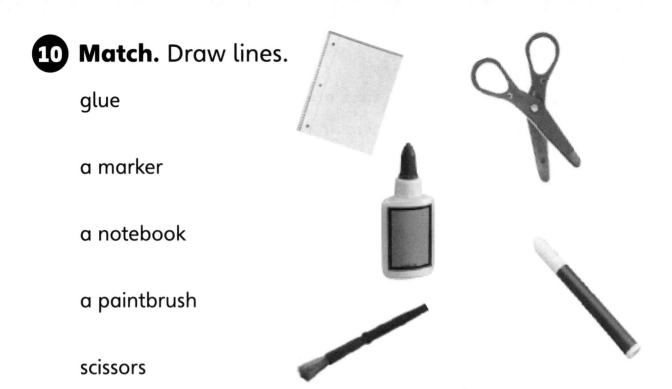

11 **Work with a partner.** Point. Talk.

What is he using?

He's using scissors.

12 **Work with a partner.** Student I, go to page II8.
Student 2, go to page I20. Take turns.

| Are there any pencils? | Yes, there are. | |
| Are there any pens? | No, there aren't. | aren't = are + not |

13 **Look, read, and write.**

1. Are there any crayons?

Yes, there are.

2. Are there any notebooks?

_____

3. Are there any markers?

_____

4. Are there any erasers?

_____

5. Are there any scissors?

_____

6. Are there any paintbrushes?

_____

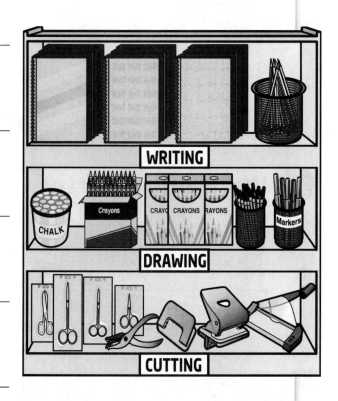

14 **Work with a partner.** Look at the picture in Activity 13. Ask and answer.

Are there any markers?

Yes, there are.

| crayons | erasers | markers | notebooks |
| paintbrushes | pencils | pens | scissors |

15 **Look.** Read and write.

1. I am d r a w i n g.

2. I am ☆ ___ ___ ___ ___ ___.

3. I am ___ ◯ ___ ___ ___ ___ ___ ___.

4. I am ___ ___ ___ ▢ ___ ___ ___.

5. I am ___ ___ ◇ ___ ___ ___.

6. I am △ ___ ___ ___ ___ ___.

16 **Read and answer.** Use the code.

What are *you* doing?

I am ▢ ☆ ◯ ▢ ◯ ◇ △ !

17 **Listen and read.** Can you say these fast? TR: 08

1. Sally's sister uses small silver scissors.

2. Green glue is on Grandmother's green gloves.

3. People paint purple paper puppets.

4. Ten turtles are talking on TV.

Mexican Yarn Paintings

This Mexican artist is painting a picture. But he is not using paint. He is not using a paintbrush! He is using beeswax and yarn. He is pressing yarn into the beeswax.

You can make a yarn painting. First, you draw a picture. You can use a pencil.

Then you use scissors to cut yarn. You can cut pieces of many colors.

Then you glue the yarn. You can use beeswax. Or, you can use glue.

19 **Choose the right answer.** Circle the answer.

1. The Mexican artist uses **beeswax and yarn.** **crayons and glue.**

2. You can use **paint.** **glue.**

Bees make their homes from beeswax. Each room is the same. Each room has six sides!

20 **Read.** Write the steps in the correct order in the boxes.

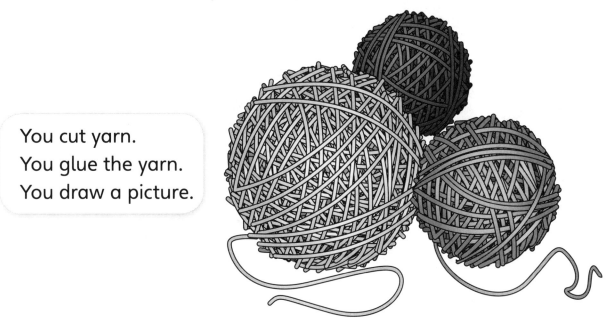

You cut yarn.
You glue the yarn.
You draw a picture.

Yarn Painting Steps

Step 1	Step 2	Step 3

21 **Work with a partner.** Think of art you like.
Tell your partner about it.

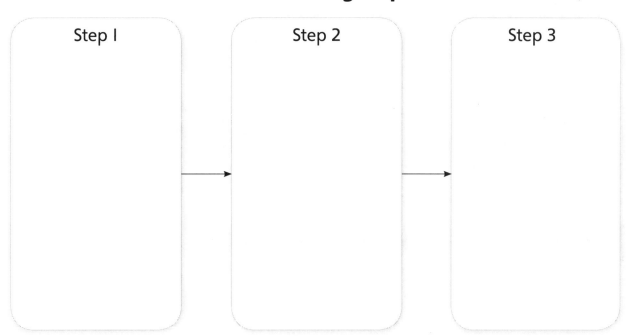

I draw pictures. I use crayons or markers.

I cut stars. I glue them on paper.

22 **Write.** What are you doing in class?

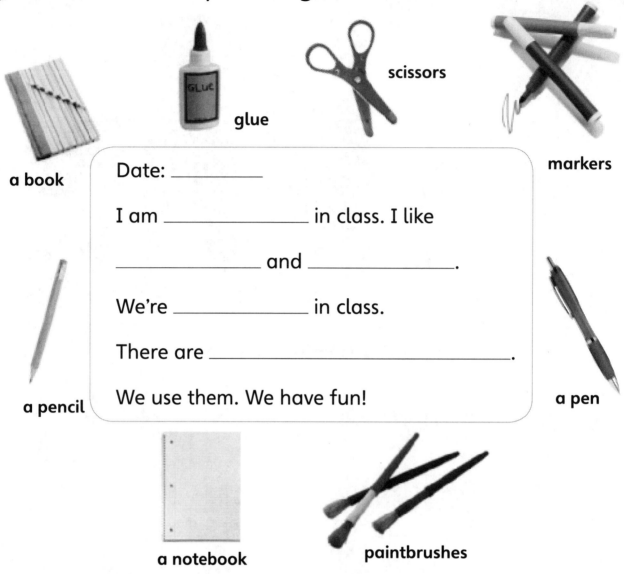

a book

glue

scissors

markers

Date: _____

I am _____ in class. I like

_____ and _____.

We're _____ in class.

There are _____.

We use them. We have fun!

a pencil

a notebook

paintbrushes

a pen

23 **What are you doing?** Write about it.
Tell what you use.

coloring   cutting   drawing   erasing
gluing   painting   writing

I am coloring. I use
markers and crayons.

_____

_____

_____

24 **Listen.** Circle the right word. **TR: 10**

I. They are **coloring / gluing**.

2. He is using **markers / scissors**.

3. I am **listening / erasing**.

4. She is **reading / writing**.

5. We are using **paintbrushes / pencils**.

25 **Look and write.** Label the things in the picture.

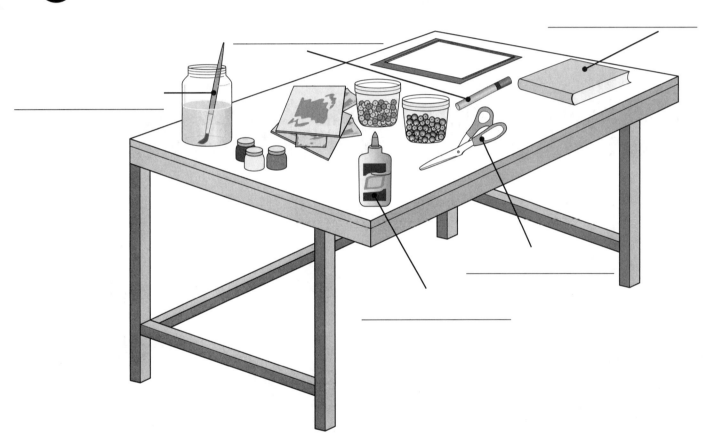

26 **Read, look, and write.** What is on the desk?

I. Are there scissors on the desk? _____

2. Are there pencils on the desk? _____

3. Are there crayons on the desk? _____

Boots and Bathing

1 **Look and write.** Use some words twice.

bathing suit	boots	gloves	hat
jacket	pants	raincoat	sweater

Cloudy and rainy?

Hot and sunny?

16

Suits

2 **Work with a partner.** Ask and answer. Take turns.

It's cloudy and rainy. What are you wearing?

I'm wearing a raincoat and boots!

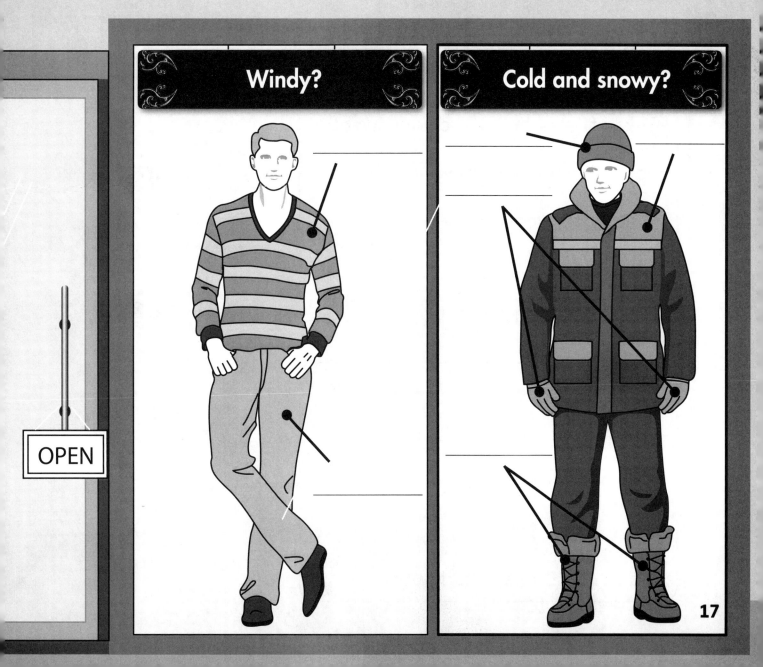

Windy?

Cold and snowy?

OPEN

3 **Listen to the song.** Read and write. TR: 11

> raincoat and pants   boots and coat
> sneakers and shorts   T-shirt and gloves

Today it's snowy.

Put on your

_____.

It's cold outside today.

Today it's sunny.

Put on your

_____.

It's hot outside today.

4 **Listen to the song.** Read and write. Match. Draw a line. TR: 12

> Take off your boots and your sweater.
>
> Take off your hat and your coat.
>
> What's the weather like?
>
> Is it _____ ? Yes!
>
> It's _____ outside today.

> Put on your boots and your sweater.
>
> Put on your hat and your coat.
>
> What's the weather like?
>
> Is it _____ ? Yes!
>
> It's _____ outside today.

GRAMMAR

What day **is it**?	**It's** Friday.	**it's** = it + is
What's the weather **like**?	**It's** rainy.	**what's** = what + is

5 **Listen, read, and write.** TR: 13

1. It's Monday. What's the weather like? It's _____.

2. It's Tuesday. What's the weather like? It's _____.

3. It's Wednesday. What's the weather like? It's _____.

1.

rainy

2.

snowy

3.

sunny

6 **Write.** Then work with a partner. Ask and answer.

	Weather	
Sunday	cloudy	It's Sunday. It's cloudy.
Monday	windy	_____
Tuesday	sunny	_____
Wednesday	snowy	_____
Thursday	rainy	_____

What day is it?   It's Monday.   What's the weather like?   It's windy.

19

7 **Look and read.** Match. Draw lines.

It's Wednesday. It's windy.

It's Thursday. It's rainy.

It's Friday. It's snowy.

8 **Can it be true?** Check **T** for *True* and **F** for *False*.

		T	F
I.	It's sunny and rainy.	Ⓣ	Ⓕ
2.	It's snowy and hot.	Ⓣ	Ⓕ
3.	It's windy and cold.	Ⓣ	Ⓕ
4.	It's cloudy and snowy.	Ⓣ	Ⓕ

9 **Write about the weather.**

_____ _____

10 **Listen.** Write. TR: 14

a coat   jeans   shorts   sneakers   an umbrella

1. It's <u>an umbrella</u>.   4. It's _____.

2. They're _____.   5. They're _____.

3. They're _____.

11 **What's missing?** Draw. Write.

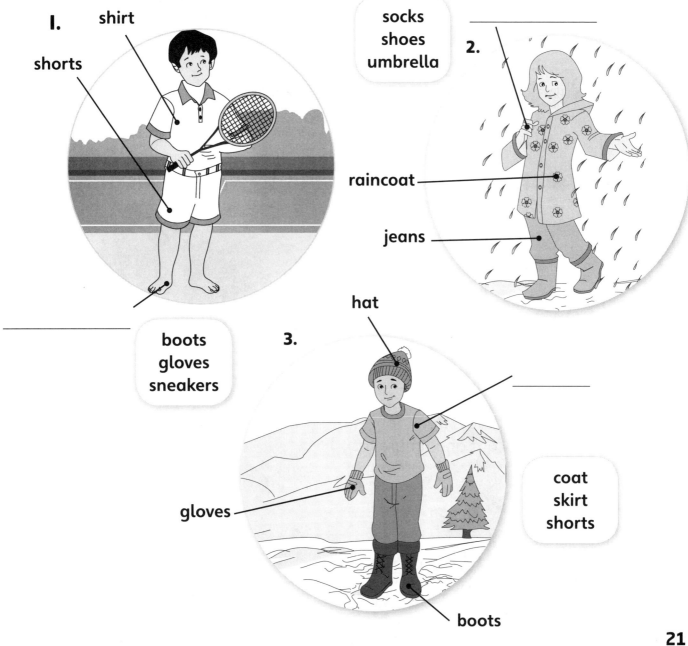

1.
shirt
shorts

socks
shoes
umbrella

2.

raincoat

jeans

boots
gloves
sneakers

hat

3.

gloves

coat
skirt
shorts

boots

It's cold	**Put on** your gloves.	it's = it + is
It's hot	**Take off** your jacket.	
It's windy.	**Don't forget** your sweater.	don't = do + not

12 **Read and write.**

1. It's hot. _____ your sweater.

2. It's rainy. _____ your umbrella.

3. It's cold. _____ your gloves.

4. It's snowy. _____ your hat.

5. It's sunny. _____ your raincoat.

13 **Work with a partner.** Tell what to wear. Take turns.

1.

3.

It's rainy today. Don't forget your raincoat and umbrella.

2.

4.

14 Read. Do the puzzles.

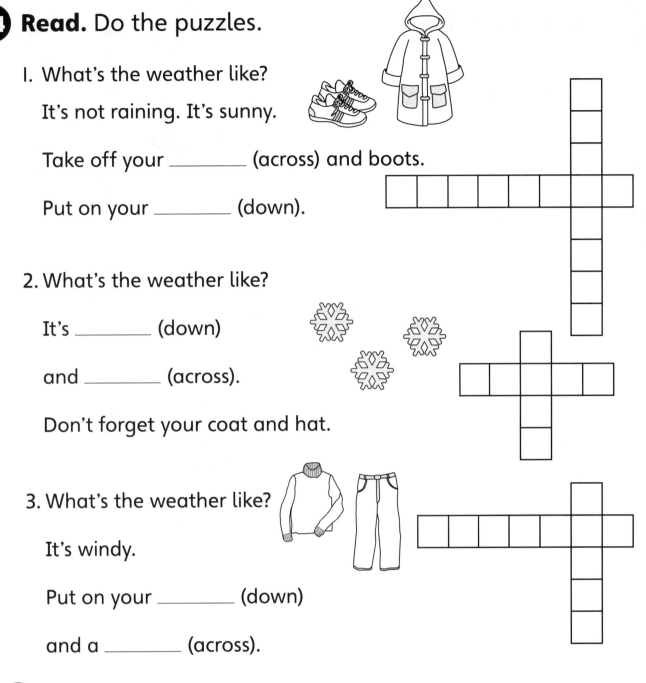

1. What's the weather like?

   It's not raining. It's sunny.

   Take off your _____ (across) and boots.

   Put on your _____ (down).

2. What's the weather like?

   It's _____ (down)

   and _____ (across).

   Don't forget your coat and hat.

3. What's the weather like?

   It's windy.

   Put on your _____ (down)

   and a _____ (across).

15 Listen and read. Can you say these fast? TR: 15

1. We have wet, windy, Wednesday weather!

2. What color coat can Cousin Cam get?

3. Suzu's sister Sada has small sweaters, socks, and shoes.

16 Work with a partner. Student 1, go to page 118. Student 2, go to page 120. Take turns.

17 **Listen and read.** TR: 16

Hats

People wear many kinds of hats. A hat keeps you warm on a cold day. You can wear a hat on a hot day. Or you can wear a hat when it's rainy. You can even wear a hat just for fun!

You can wear a hard hat. It keeps you safe. You can wear a work hat. It shows what your job is. You can wear a hat just one time!

People all around the world wear hats. What hats do you wear? Why?

18 **Read.** Check **T** for *True* and **F** for *False*.

1. Hats can keep you warm. Ⓣ Ⓕ

2. People wear hats just for work. Ⓣ Ⓕ

3. You can wear a hat just one time. Ⓣ Ⓕ

19 **Work with a partner.** Look and read. Talk about hats.

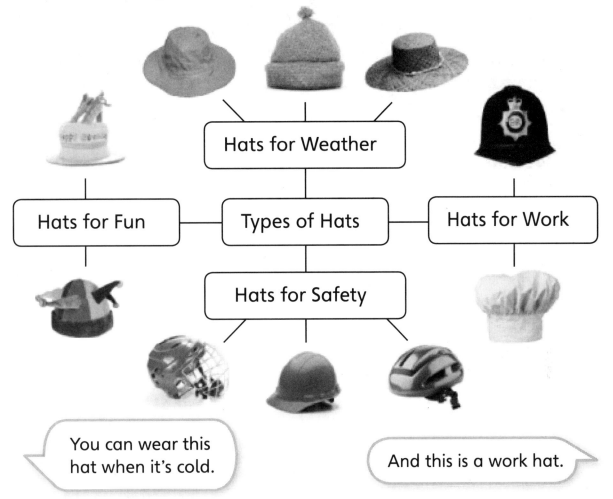

Hats for Weather

Hats for Fun — Types of Hats — Hats for Work

Hats for Safety

You can wear this hat when it's cold.

And this is a work hat.

20 **Look and read.** Match. Write the letter.

a

b

c

d

1. It's sunny. _____   3. Let's ride bikes! _____

2. It's cold. _____   4. It's raining. _____

21 **Write.** Write about your favorite hat.

1. What color is your hat? _____

2. When do you wear your hat? _____

22 **Read and check.**

What do you wear?

	boots	gloves	raincoat	shorts	sweater	T-shirt
It's sunny.						
It's rainy.						
It's cold.						

23 **Choose a place.** Write about the weather. Tell what to wear. Use words from the box.

boots	cold	a raincoat	sneakers	a sweater
cloudy	hot	rainy	snowy	an umbrella
a coat	jeans	shorts	sunny	windy

_____

_____

_____

_____

_____

It's windy here!
Put on jeans and
sneakers. Don't
forget your
sweater.

24 **What's the weather like?** It's windy! Find things to wear. Color and write.

I see six things to wear. They are _____,

_____, _____, _____,

_____, and _____.

25 **Read and write.** Tell what to wear. Use words from the box.

> Don't forget   Put on   Take off

1. It's cold. _____.

2. It's windy. _____.

3. It's hot. _____.

Unit 3

Fun in the Sun

1 **Look and write.** _____

fly a kite	jump rope
play baseball	play basketball
play hide and seek	play soccer
ride a bike	rollerblade
skateboard	play a game

_____

_____

2 **Work with a partner.**
Point. Ask and answer.

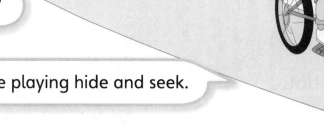

What are they doing?

They're playing hide and seek.

3 **Match.** Draw lines.

I. I like to 🚲 .

Yes, I do. Yes, I do.

2. I like to 🪁 .

Yes, I do. Yes, I do.

3. I like to ▦ .

I like to play outside with you.

4. I like to 〰 .

Yes, I do. Yes, I do.

5. I like to 🛼 .

Yes, I do. Yes, I do.

6. I like to ⚽ .

I like to play with you.

climb a tree

rollerblade

play games

swim

ride a bike

skateboard

play baseball

fly a kite

jump rope

play soccer

4 **Listen to the song.** Check your answers. TR: 17

5 **What do you like to do outside?** Read and write. Sing.

I like to _____ .

Yes, I do. Yes, I do.

I like to _____ .

Yes, I do. Yes, I do.

I like to _____ .

I like to play outside with you.

It's fun, fun, fun!

Do you **like to** play soccer?   Yes, I do. It's fun.   it's = it + is

Do you **like to** rollerblade?   No, I don't. It's boring.   don't = do not

What do you **like to do**?   I **like to play** soccer.

What do they **like to do**?   They **like to rollerblade.**

6 **Look and listen.** Write numbers. TR: 18

7 **Work with a partner.** Ask and answer.

Do you like to play basketball?

No, I don't. It's boring.

31

8 **Look and listen.** Check **T** for *True* and **F** for *False*. TR: 19

1. Manuel likes to skateboard. Ⓣ Ⓕ
2. Manuel likes to jump rope. Ⓣ Ⓕ
3. Manuel likes to play baseball. Ⓣ Ⓕ

9 **Listen again.** Read and write. What does Manuel like? TR: 20

boring   fun

1. Manuel, do you like to play baseball?

   " Yes, I do. It's fun! _____ "

2. Do you like to jump rope?

   " _____ "

3. Do you like to skateboard?

   " _____ "

10 **Write.** Make two lists.

I like to...	I don't like to...

11 **Work with a partner.** Talk about your lists.

What do you like to do?

I like to play soccer.

Do you like to play basketball?

No, I don't. It's boring.

12 **Listen and write.** Number the pictures. TR: 21

13 **What do you like to do?** Check ✓ if you like it.
Write ✗ if you don't like it.

bounce a ball	
catch a ball	
play tag	
throw a ball	
watch a game	

14 **Write about your chart.**

1. I _____. It's _____.

2. I don't _____. It's _____.

Let's watch a game.   Sure. That sounds like fun.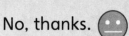

Let's play tag.   No, thanks. 😐

let's = let us

15 **Read, write, and color.** What do you think?

Let's throw a ball.   _____ skateboard.   _____ play hide and seek.

😊 😐

😊 😐

😊 😐

_____ bounce a ball.   _____ fly a kite.   _____ rollerblade.

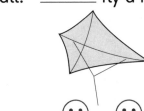

😊 😐

😊 😐

😊 😐

_____ play soccer.   _____ jump rope.   _____ catch a ball.

😊 😐

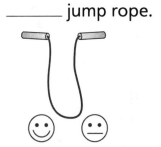

😊 😐

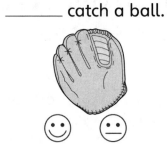

😊 😐

16 **Work with a partner.** Talk about the activities.

Let's throw a ball.   No, thanks.

17 **Choose three** 😊. Write about them.

Let's _____, _____, and _____.

34

18 **Listen and draw.** Draw a line from START to END. TR: 22

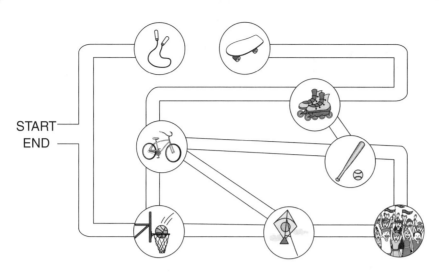

19 **Read.** Choose. Write what you like 🙂.

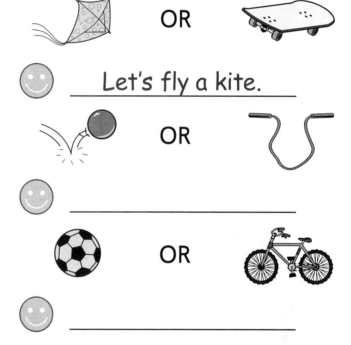

OR

🙂 _Let's fly a kite._

OR

🙂 _____

OR

🙂 _____

20 **Work with a partner.** Student I, go to page II9. Student 2, go to page I2I. Take turns.

21 **Listen and read.** Can you say these fast? TR: 23

1. Big boys bounce basketballs.

2. Six silly soccer stars skateboard.

3. Rollerbladers race through Rome.

Listen and read. TR: 24

The X Games

People all around the world like to watch the X Games. The X Games take place in hot weather and cold weather.

ski

Hot Weather
The players like to skateboard, ride bikes, and race cars. The players like to go fast. They like to do tricks.

Cold Weather
The players like the snow. They ski and snowboard. They ride snowmobiles. They go fast. They do tricks.

Do you like to watch TV? Watch the X Games!

ride snowmobiles

skateboard

ride bikes

race cars

snowboard

23 **Read.** Check **T** for *True* and **F** for *False*.

1. They play the X Games only in hot weather.   ⓣ   ⓕ

2. X Games players like to do tricks.   ⓣ   ⓕ

3. Players skateboard in cold weather.   ⓣ   ⓕ

4. You can watch the X Games on TV.   ⓣ   ⓕ

24 **Write about the X Games.**

The X Games

Hot Weather

skateboard

_____

_____

Hot and Cold Weather

go fast

_____

_____

Cold Weather

ski _____

_____

_____

25 **Look, read, and write.**

1. He's in the X Games.

The weather is _____.

He likes to ride _____.

2. She's in the X Games.

The weather is _____.

She likes to ride _____.

26 **You are in the X Games!** Draw and write.

I am in the X Games.

The weather is _____.

I like _____

_____.

Read. Look at the pictures. Match.

I like to play soccer. I like to run and kick the ball!

My name is Sada. I like to ride my bike.

28 **Draw and write.** It's sunny! What do you like to do?

_____   _____

_____   _____

_____   _____

_____   _____

29 **Play a game.** Find people doing fun things.
Color and write.

People like to _____fly a kite_____, _____,

_____, _____, and _____.

30 **Read and write.**

1. Do you like to ride a bike?

_____

2. What do you like to ride?

_____

3. What do you like to do with a ball?

_____

31 **Work with a partner.** Ask and answer. Do you
like the same things?

Let's play baseball.

No, thanks. It's boring.

Review

1 **Look.** Read. Underline the correct answer.

1. What are you doing?

   We're **counting. / talking.**

2. What are you doing?

   I'm **gluing. / coloring.**

   I'm using **a marker. / glue.**

3. What are you doing?

   We're **writing. / drawing.**

4. What are you doing?

   I'm **gluing paper. / cutting paper.**

   I'm using **glue. / scissors.**

2 **Read.** Look at page 40. Write.

1. Are there any notebooks? ___Yes, there are.___

2. Are there any scissors? _____

3. Are there any hats? _____

4. Are there any shorts? _____

3 **What's the weather like?** Read. Underline the correct answer.

1.

It's **windy. / rainy.**

Take off / Put on your raincoat.

Don't forget your **shorts. / umbrella.**

2.

It's **cloudy. / sunny.**

Take off / Put on your sweater.

Put on your **bathing suit. / coat.**

4 **Listen.** Read. Match. Draw a line. TR: 25

1. Do you like to skateboard?   a. I like to play tag.

2. What do they like to do?   b. Sure. That sounds like fun!

3. Do you like to bounce a ball?   c. They like to rollerblade.

4. What do you like to do?   d. Yes, I do. It's fun.

5. Let's play a game.   e. No, I don't. It's boring.

6. Let's watch a game.   f. No, thanks.

41

Unit 4

Inside Our House

1 **Look and write.**

an armchair
a bed
a bookcase
a fireplace
a lamp
a microwave
a picture
a rug
shelves
a shower
stairs
a stove
a table
a tub

_____

_____

_____

2 Work with a partner. Ask and answer.

Is there a microwave in the kitchen?

No, there isn't.

_____

_____

_____

_____

_____

_____

3 Listen and write numbers. TR: 26

☐ Is there food in there?

☐ This is where I live.

1 Welcome to my house.

☐ Welcome to my kitchen.

☐ May I try some?
May I, please?

☐ Something's cooking on the stove.

☐ There's lots of food inside.

☐ The refrigerator is between the windows.

4 Write a new verse for the song. Use some words from the box.

| armchair | bathroom | bed | bedroom | bookcase |
| living room | rug | shower | sofa | tub |

Where is the _____? It's in the _____.

Where is the _____? It's in the _____.

Where is the _____? It's in the _____.

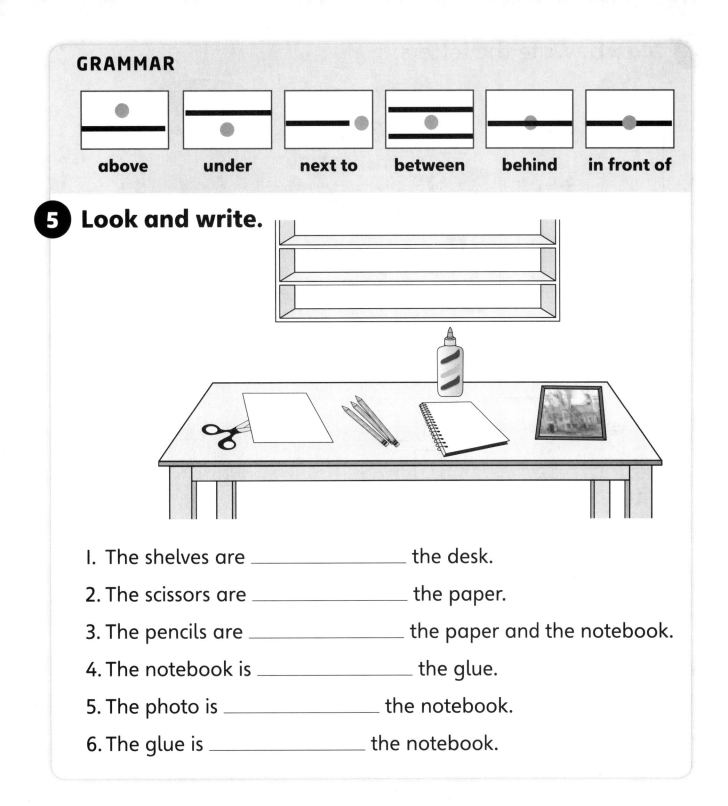

above   under   next to   between   behind   in front of

5 **Look and write.**

1. The shelves are _____ the desk.

2. The scissors are _____ the paper.

3. The pencils are _____ the paper and the notebook.

4. The notebook is _____ the glue.

5. The photo is _____ the notebook.

6. The glue is _____ the notebook.

6 **Work with a partner.** Put things on your desk.
Ask and answer.

Where are the pencils?   They're next to the notebook.

7 **Match.** Write the letters.

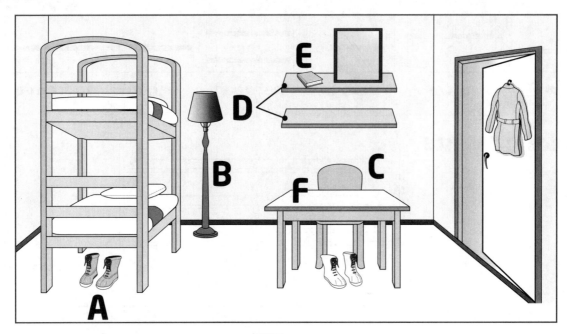

1. They're under the beds. ☐

2. It's next to the mirror. ☐

3. They're above the desk. ☐

4. It's in front of the chair. ☐

5. It's between the desk and the bed. ☐

6. It's behind the desk. ☐

8 **Listen and do.** TR: 27

9 **Listen and** circle. TR: 28

1. The armchair is   **next to / in front of**   the fireplace.

2. The rug is   **in front of / next to**   the tub.

3. The shelves are   **under / above**   the stove.

4. The bookcase is   **behind / between**   the stairs and
   the armchair.

10 **Read and match.** Draw lines.

1. The refrigerator is next to the stove.

2. The window is next to the stove.

3. The stove is next to the sink.

4. The phone is next to the stove.

5. The stove is next to the door.

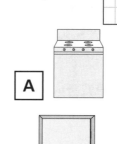
A

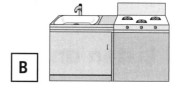
B

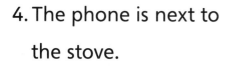
C

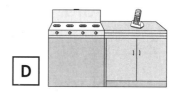
D

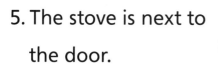
E

11 **Look and write.**

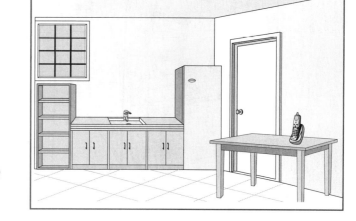

1. There is a _____ above the shelves.

2. The _____ is between the shelves and the refrigerator.

3. The _____ is on the table.

4. There is a _____ between the sink and the door.

12 **Work with a partner.** Ask and answer.

What's above the shelves?

The window is above the shelves.

13 **Listen and answer.** TR: 29

1. _____ in front of the sofa.

2. _____ next to the fireplace.

3. _____ between the armchairs.

4. _____ above the fireplace.

14 **Look at the picture.** Read and write.

1. Where is the lamp?

   <u>It's</u> behind an armchair.

2. Where is the window?

   _____ above the sofa.

3. Where is the rug?

   _____ in front of the fireplace.

4. Where are the photos?

   _____ on the shelves.

15 Do the puzzle.

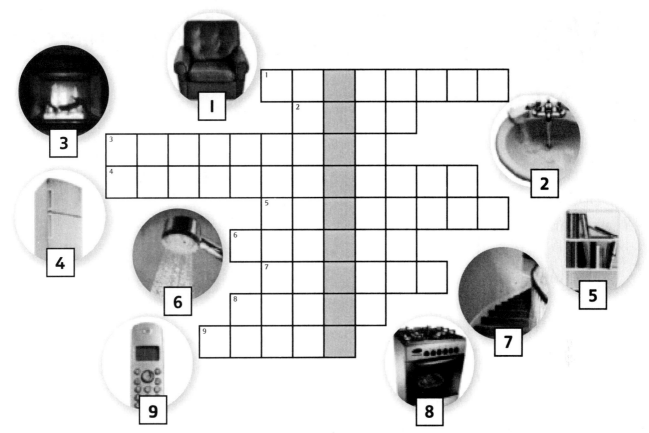

16 Look at the puzzle. Read and write.

Look at the gray squares. Read the word from top to bottom.

What is the word? _____

17 Listen and read. Can you say these fast? TR: 30

1. There aren't any shelves in the shower.

2. Take the stove up the stairs.

3. Next to the window, behind the door, under the table, above the floor.

18 Work with a partner. Student 1, go to page 119.
Student 2, go to page 122. Take turns.

Welcome to Our Houses

An Apartment

Alice and her family live in an apartment. There are two bedrooms. Her parents' bedroom is next to the bathroom. Alice and her sister share a bedroom. The kitchen is between the living room and Alice's bedroom. The apartment is in a big building. There are other apartments in the building. Other people live in those apartments.

an apartment

Many apartments are in this building.

A Mobile Home

Ben's family lives in a mobile home in the summer. There is a bathroom with a shower. There isn't a tub. There's a living room. There's a table and four chairs in the living room. There isn't a door to the kitchen, but there's a stove, a sink, a refrigerator, and a microwave. Ben's parents drive the mobile home to new places. Ben's family has lots of fun!

mobile homes

20 **Read and match.** Draw lines.

1. In Alice's apartment there are two   a. tub.

2. The apartment is in a   b. shower.

3. In Ben's mobile home there isn't a   c. building.

4. In Ben's mobile home there is a   d. bedrooms.

21 **Read and write.**

1. How many bedrooms are in Alice's apartment?

   _____

2. Can Ben's parents drive the mobile home? _____

3. Is the apartment in a building? _____

4. Is the mobile home in a building? _____

22 **Work with a partner.** Look and read. Talk about Alice's apartment and Ben's mobile home.

Houses

Alice's Apartment	**Both**	**Ben's Mobile Home**
in a building two bedrooms	a kitchen a bathroom a living room	can drive it not in a building has a shower no tub

This house in Poland looks like it's melting.

51

23 **Choose a room.** Write about it. Use words from the box.

| armchair | bed | bookcase | fireplace | lamp | mirror | rug |
| shelves | shower | stairs | teddy bear | tub | window |

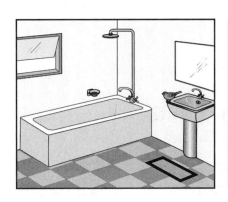  

1. Room: _____

2. What is in the room?

_____

_____

24 **Draw and write.** Draw a house you want. Write about it.

1. My house is _____.

2. It has _____ windows.

3. My house has these rooms: _____

_____ .

4. A _____ is in the _____ .

52

25 **Find and color.**

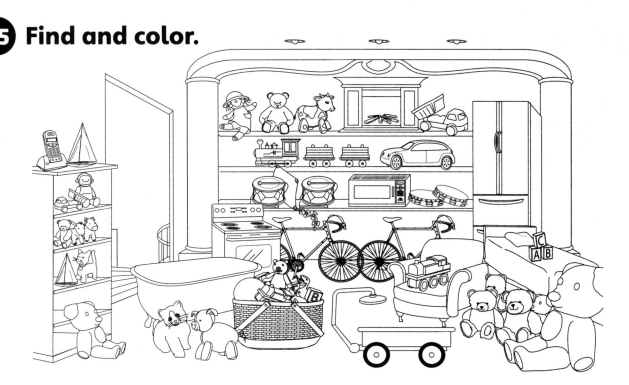

Find a stove, a refrigerator, a phone, a microwave, a shower, a tub, a bookcase, a bed, a fireplace, and an armchair.

26 **Look at the picture.** Read and write. Use words from the box.

above	behind	in front of	between
It's	next to	They're	under

1. Where is the doll?

   <u>It's next to the teddy bear.</u>

2. Where is the door?

   _____

3. Where are the shelves?

   _____

4. Where is the kite?

   _____

Unit 5

Day by Day

1 **Look and match.** Write the number.

1

2

3

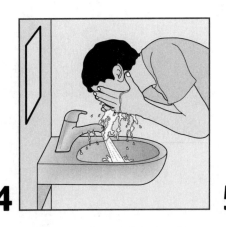

4

5

6

7

8

9

10

11

☐ I get up.	☐ I get dressed.	☐ I eat breakfast.
☐ I eat lunch.	☐ I eat dinner.	☐ I go to school.
☐ I go to bed.	☐ I wash my face.	☐ I brush my teeth.
☐ I play with friends.	☐ I play video games.	

2 **Work with a partner.** Ask and answer. Point. Take turns.

> Who is getting dressed?

> He is getting dressed.

3 **Listen to the song.** Write. Read. Draw lines to match. TR: 32

1. It's _____ o'clock.

   It's _____ o'clock.

   It's _____ o'clock in the morning.

   I _____ at _____ o'clock.

   I always _____ at _____.

2. It's _____ o'clock.

   It's _____ o'clock.

   It's _____ o'clock in the afternoon.

   I always _____ at

   _____ o'clock.

   I _____ every day.

4 **Write a new verse for the song!** Use some words from the box.

eleven	five	four	morning
afternoon	play video games	wash my face	six
take a bath	get dressed	one	read a book

It's _____ o'clock. It's _____ o'clock.

It's _____ o'clock in the _____.

I always _____ at _____ every day.

I _____ at _____ every day.

What time is it?   **It's** 4:00.   It's four **o'clock**.
When do you go to school?   **At** 8:00.   At eight **o'clock**.   **It's** = It is
When does she eat dinner?   **At** 6:00.   At six **o'clock**.

5 **Read, look, and match.** Draw lines.

1. It's one o'clock.

2. It's seven o'clock.

3. It's five o'clock.

4. It's twelve o'clock.

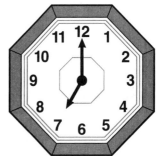

5. It's nine o'clock.

6 **Listen and write.** TR: 33

1. _____ is it?

2. _____ do you eat lunch?

3. _____ is it?

4. _____ does he play with his friends?

5. _____ does she go to bed?

7 **Listen and (circle.)** TR: 34

1. At two o'clock.   It's two o'clock.

2. At 1:00.   It's 1:00.

3. It's 3:00.   At 3:00.

4. It's four o'clock.   At four o'clock.

5. It's 9:00.   At 9:00.

8 **Read and write.** Choose a word from the box.

at   it's

1. I get up _____ seven o'clock.

2. _____ one o'clock. I'm eating lunch.

3. I go to school _____ eight o'clock.

4. _____ nine o'clock. I'm going to bed.

9 **Work with a partner.** Fill in the chart.
Write the times.

	When do you...?	When does your partner...?
get up		
eat breakfast		
go to school		
eat lunch		

10 **Work with a partner.** Student 1, go to page 121.
Student 2, go to page 122. Take turns.

11 **Read and look.** Match. Draw lines.

1. We go to bed at night.

2. We go to school in the morning.

3. We watch TV in the evening.

4. We play in the park in the afternoon.

12 **Read and write.**

1. School starts at eight o'clock. Gracia goes to school at seven o'clock. Juan goes to school at ten o'clock. Who's late for school?

_____

2. My family eats dinner at six o'clock. My father gets home at five o'clock. My sister Gina gets home at seven o'clock. Who's late for dinner?

_____

What do you do **every day**? I **always** take a bath.

What does your sister do in the morning?

She reads. She **never** plays video games in the morning.

13 **Read and match.** Write. What do you always do? What do you never do? Compare your sentences to a partner's.

I	always never	go play eat	lunch to school to bed breakfast with friends video games	in the morning. in the afternoon. in the evening. at night.

1. I never go to bed in the morning.

2. _____

3. _____

4. _____

14 **Draw and write.** What do you do every day?

I _____

every day.

15 Look and write.

1 ✓

2 ✗

3 ✓

4 ✗

5 ✓

X = never
✓ = every day

1. He washes his face every day.

2. _____

3. _____

4. _____

5. _____

16 Look and read. Write what the dog says.

What time is it?

It's time for lunch!

17 Listen and read. Can you say these fast? TR: 35

1. We always play in the park.

2. Never bounce a ball in the bathroom.

3. Eat an apple every night at eight o'clock.

Tubby the Labrador

Dog Helps Planet

This is Tubby the Labrador. He's a smart dog! We all know recycling is a good idea, and Tubby knows it, too. Tubby recycles plastic bottles. Every day he goes to the park for a walk. Other dogs like to play with a ball, but Tubby never plays with a ball. Tubby always picks up plastic bottles. Tubby's owner takes the plastic bottles to the recycling center. Tubby picks up many plastic bottles every day! Tubby helps to keep the park clean.

19 **Read.** Check **T** for *True* and **F** for *False*.

1. Tubby goes to the park every day. Ⓣ Ⓕ

2. Tubby likes to play ball. Ⓣ Ⓕ

3. Tubby likes to pick up plastic bottles. Ⓣ Ⓕ

20 **Look and read.** Work with a partner. Talk about dogs.

Tubby
- picks up plastic bottles
- recycles

Both
- go to the park

Other dogs
- play with a ball

21 **Read and write.**

1. Where do Tubby and the dogs go?

_____

2. What do the other dogs do?

_____

3. Does Tubby play with a ball?

_____

4. What does Tubby pick up?

_____

22 **Choose a time of day.** What do you do? Write.
Use some words from the box.

in the morning	in the afternoon	in the evening
at seven o'clock	at twelve o'clock	at six o'clock
at eight o'clock	at two o'clock	at seven o'clock
at eleven o'clock	at three o'clock	always
always	always	every
every	every	

I wake up at seven o'clock.

_____

_____

_____

_____

23 **Write.** What do you like to do every day?

In the morning, I like to _____.

In the afternoon, I like to _____.

In the evening, I like to _____.

At night, I like to _____.

24 Listen and draw a line. TR: 37

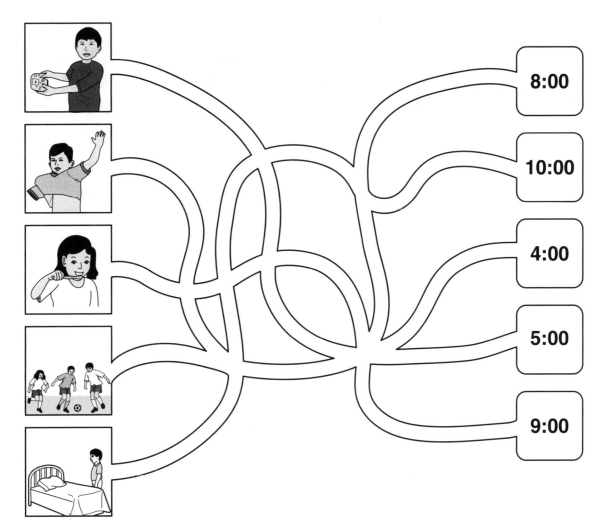

25 Read and write.

1. What do you do every Monday night?

_____

2. What do you always do on Wednesday mornings?

_____

3. What do you never do on Sunday?

_____

Unit 6

How Are You?

1 **Look and write.**

angry	bored	excited	hungry
scared	silly	surprised	sad
tired	happy	worried	thirsty

1 ___happy___

3 _____

10 _____

2 ___sad___

66

2 **Read and match.** Draw lines.

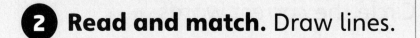

1. I'm tired. What can I do?
2. I'm hungry. What can I do?
3. I'm bored. What can I do?

a. I can play a game.
b. I can go to bed.
c. I can eat lunch.

HAPPY BIRTHDAY

6 _____

4 _____

12 _____

7 _____

5 _____

8 _____

9 _____

11 _____

3 **Listen and choose.** Circle the correct words. TR: 38

1. Sometimes I'm **angry / excited.**

   Sometimes I'm just **tired / bored.**

   Sometimes I'm **excited / hungry.**

2. Sometimes I'm **worried / smiling.**

   I'm **laughing / crying** at a joke!

   Sometimes I'm **angry / crying.**

   I feel **bored / sad.**

4 **Listen and write.** TR: 39

Sometimes I'm _____.

Sometimes I'm _____.

Sometimes I'm feeling _____.

scared
tired
worried

5 **Write a new verse for the song!** Use some words from the box. Read your writing to a partner.

angry	bored	excited	hungry	scared
silly	surprised	thirsty	tired	worried

It's OK to be _____,

or sometimes to feel _____.

It's OK to be _____,

or sometimes to feel _____.

68

GRAMMAR

How are you?	I'm **OK**. 😐
	I'm **fine**. 🙂
	I'm **great**! 😀
	We're **great**! 😀
You **look** tired.	Yes. I'm tired.
	No. We're bored.
She **looks** scared.	No. She's surprised.
He **looks** tired.	Yes. He's tired.
They **look** angry.	No. They're bored.

6 **Read.** Look at the pictures. Match.

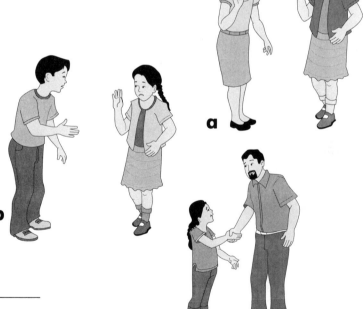

1. How are you?

   I'm great! _____

2. How are you?

   I'm fine. _____

3. How are you?

   I'm okay. I'm tired. _____

7 **Listen and write.** TR: 40

1. I'm _____.

2. I'm _____!

3. _____?

4. We're _____.

69

8 **Write sentences.** Write the words in the correct order.

1. you? / How / are _____

2. great! / I'm _____

3. OK. / We're _____

4. am / I / fine. _____

9 **Look and write.** How do they look? Use some words from the box.

| angry | bored | excited | hungry | scared |
| surprised | thirsty | tired | worried | |

1. <u>She looks hungry.</u>

2. _____

3. _____

4. _____

5. _____

6. _____

10 Read. Look at the pictures. Match.

a

c

b

e

d

1. He's crying. _____

2. She's laughing. _____

3. He's smiling. _____

4. She's yawning. _____

5. He's frowning. _____

11 Listen and write. TR: 41

1. The girl is happy. She's _____.

2. My sister is _____. She feels sad.

3. The boy is _____. He's worried.

4. It's fun to play! My friends are _____.

5. My brother is tired. He's _____.

12 Work with a partner. Student 1, go to page 123.
Student 2, go to page 124. Take turns.

GRAMMAR

shelf	**shelves**	There are three **shelves** above the desk.
tooth	**teeth**	I brush my **teeth** every day.
foot	**feet**	You put socks and shoes on your **feet**.
person	**people**	The **people** are laughing.
child	**children**	Some **children** are reading books.
sheep	**sheep**	Two **sheep** are eating.

13 Read and write.

1. My rabbit has two big _____. (tooth)

2. There are toys and books on the _____ in my room. (shelf)

3. There are ten _____ on the train. (person)

4. I like to play hide and seek with my _____. (friend)

14 Work with a partner. Read and write. Find and color.

1. Find two ___gloves___. (glove)

2. Find a dog wearing boots on its _____. (foot)

3. Find three _____. (sheep)

72

15 Find the words. Circle the words.

| angry | bored | excited | hungry | scared | silly | surprised | thirsty | tired | worried |

t	i	r	e	d	p	z	x	b
h	u	n	g	r	y	m	m	o
i	l	l	r	a	d	r	s	r
r	s	t	y	o	r	e	p	e
s	u	r	p	r	i	s	e	d
t	u	w	v	e	f	i	x	r
y	b	s	a	n	l	l	c	y
z	t	c	n	i	o	l	i	o
b	o	a	g	t	i	y	t	l
w	o	r	r	i	e	d	e	p
s	c	e	y	f	l	a	d	p
a	n	d	o	h	u	p	p	y

16 Read. Draw the faces.

1. crying

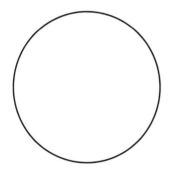

2. laughing

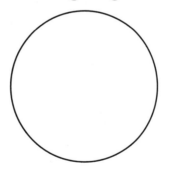

3. frowning

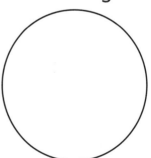

17 Listen and read. Can you say these fast? TR: 42

1. Four yawning boys bounce balls.

2. Five frowning frogs fly kites.

3. Six smiling sisters see six sheep.

4. Seven crying children count crayons.

Clowns

People see clowns at the circus. Clowns do silly things. They climb ladders and fall down. They drive tiny cars and make noises. Clowns spill water. They get wet.

Many people like to watch clowns. Clowns surprise people. Many people laugh when they watch clowns.

Clowns wear silly clothes. They paint their faces. Some clowns have happy faces. They are smiling. Some clowns have sad faces. This clown looks sad.

Some people feel scared when they see clowns. Why? Some clowns are big. Their painted faces are strange!

19 **Read.** Check **T** for *True* or **F** for *False*.

1. Clowns do silly things.   T   F

2. People see clowns at baseball games.   T   F

3. Some clowns have happy faces.   T   F

20 **Read and write.** Work with a partner. Talk about clowns.

surprise people:
• make people laugh

scare some people:
• are big
• have strange _____

do silly things:
• climb ladders
• fall _____
• drive tiny _____
• make noises
• spill _____
• get wet

clowns

wear silly clothes and paint their faces:
• look happy
• are _____
• look _____
• look strange

21 **Read and write.**

1. What silly things can clowns do?

_____

_____

2. Do clowns always have happy faces?

_____

3. Why do some people feel scared when they see clowns?

_____

22 **What about you?** Read. Circle. Write.

I **like / don't like** clowns. Why?

I am _____ when I see clowns.

23 **Look.** Read and write.

I. There are two _____ with their father.

2. Two _____ are laughing. Their friend is _____.

3. The mother is eating. She looks _____. Her dog

    looks _____.

4. The rabbit has one big _____.

5. The baby is wearing a sock on one _____.

In this picture...

6. There is one _____ with the father.

7. One child is _____. Two _____ are crying.

8. The mother is yawning. She looks _____.

    Her dog looks _____.

9. The rabbit has three big _____.

10. The baby is wearing socks on two _____.

24 **Draw and write.** You are playing a game. Who is playing with you? How do you feel?

_____

_____

_____

_____

1 **Look.** Read and write. Use words from the box.

above   behind   between   in front of
It's   next to   They're   under

1. Where is the refrigerator?

   ___It's___ ___next to___ the sink.

2. Where is the bookcase?

   _____ _____ the armchairs.

3. Where are the shelves?

   _____ _____ the stove.

4. Where is the rug?

   _____ _____ the fireplace.

5. Where are the armchairs?

   _____ _____ the window.

2 **Read.** Look at the pictures. Match.

a

b
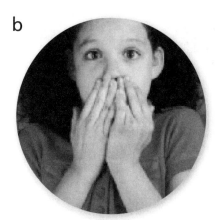

c

1. She looks tired. She's yawning. _____

2. She looks angry. She's frowning. _____

3. She looks surprised. No, she's scared. _____

3 **Listen and circle.** TR: 44

1. I'm OK.   I'm great!

2. At 8:00.   It's 8:00.

3. When do you eat dinner?   When do you eat lunch?

4. At six o'clock.   It's six o'clock.

5. What do you never do?   What do you do every day?

4 **Read and write.**

1. It's 12:00. The _____ are hungry. (child)

2. Some _____ go to school at night. (person)

3. Do you like to play video _____? (game)

4. I always brush my _____ at night. (tooth)

Unit 7

Awesome Animals

_____

1 **Look and write.**

> camel   crocodile   elephant   giraffe
>
> hippo   kangaroo   lion   monkey
>
> panda   parrot   penguin   tiger   zebra

_____

2 **Work with a partner.**
Point. Ask and answer.

> What is this?

> It's a parrot!

_____   _____   _____

_____   _____

_____   _____   _____

_____   _____   _____

3 **Listen to the song.** Write. Use words from the box. Draw lines to match. **TR: 45**

kangaroo   monkey   parrot   penguin

A _____ is a bird that flies.

It can't swim, but it can fly.

A _____ swings from

tree to tree, tree to tree, tree to tree.

A _____ is a bird that swims.

It can't fly, but it can swim.

A _____ can hop and jump.

It can't climb, but it can jump.

4 **Write a new verse for the song!**
Use some words from the box.

A _____ is an animal

that _____.

It can't _____, but it can

_____.

A _____ is an animal

that _____.

camel	climb
hippo	crawl
lion	hop
tiger	jump
turtle	run
zebra	swim
	swing
	walk

GRAMMAR

Can a tiger climb a tree?	Yes, it **can**. It **can** climb a tree.
Can a tiger fly?	No, it **can't**. It **can't** fly.
Can tigers climb trees?	Yes, they **can**. They **can** climb trees.
Can tigers fly?	No, they **can't**. They **can't** fly.

can't = cannot

5 **Read and match.** Write true sentences. Compare your sentences to a partner's. Are they all true?

A hippo A parrot A panda Monkeys Crocodiles Kangaroos	can can't	jump. run. hop. fly. walk. climb.

1. <u>A hippo can't climb.</u>

2. _____

3. _____

4. _____

5. _____

6 **Listen and check.** What can Sofia and Marcos do? TR: 46

	jump	walk	run	climb
Sofia				
Marcos				

7 **What about Sonia and her family?** Write what they can and can't do.

climb a tree   ~~play basketball~~
~~cook~~   play soccer
do a puzzle   walk

1. Sonia <u>can play basketball</u>, but she

    <u>can't cook</u>.

2. Her brother _____ , but he

    _____.

3. Her baby sister _____, but she

    _____.

8 **What about you?** Write two things you can and can't do.

1. I _____, but I _____.

2. I _____, but I _____.

84

9 **What can you say?** Circle all the correct letters.

1. long _____
   a. trunk   b. hair   c. neck   d. apple

2. sharp _____
   a. jacket   b. claws   c. teeth   d. pencil

3. short _____
   a. tail   b. ball   c. clock   d. legs

4. colorful _____
   a. dress   b. crayons   c. feathers   d. kite

5. big _____
   a. teeth   b. armchair   c. glue   d. ears

10 **Look at the animals.** Write.

1   A penguin has small eyes. _____

2. _____

3. _____

4. _____

5. _____

Does a panda **have** a short tail?	Yes, it **does**.	**doesn't** = does not
Does a panda **have** a long neck?	No, it **doesn't**.	
Do pandas **have** short tails?	Yes, they **do**.	**don't** = do not
Do pandas **have** long necks?	No, they **don't**.	

11 **Read and write.** Work with a partner. Ask and answer.

1. <u>Does</u> a crocodile <u>have sharp teeth</u> ?

   <u>Yes, it does.</u> .

2. _____ a monkey _____ ?

   _____ .

3. _____ an elephant _____ ?

   _____ .

4. _____ penguins _____ ?

   _____ .

5. _____ giraffes _____ ?

   _____ .

12 **Listen and answer.** Then listen again and write. TR: 47

1. _____   3. _____

2. _____   4. _____

13 **Draw a new animal.** Work with a partner.
Talk about your animals.

14 **Work with a partner.** Student I, go to page 123.
Student 2, go to page 124. Take turns.

15 **Listen and Read.** Can you say these fast? TR: 48

1. eleven elegant elephants

2. zany zebras zig and zag

3. five fat friendly frogs

4. happy heavy hippos

16 Listen and read. TR: 49

Camels Are Cool!

Camels are awesome animals. They are big and strong and live to be 40 to 50 years old. They live in very, very hot and dry places. Bactrian camels live in rocky deserts in Asia. Arabian camels live in sandy deserts in North Africa.

Bactrian camels have two humps, but Arabian camels have just one hump. All camels can go without food and water for a long time. Their humps help them do this.

When it is windy, camels can protect their eyes. They have three eyelids on each eye and two sets of long eyelashes. And when sand and dirt are blowing everywhere, they can close up their noses, too!

Arabian camel

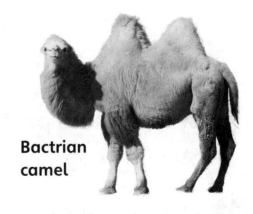

Bactrian camel

17 Match the sentence parts. Draw lines.

1. Camels live

2. Camels can have

3. Camels can protect

a. their eyes from wind and sand.

b. in very hot and dry places.

c. one or two humps.

18 **Look and read.** Work with a partner.
Talk about camels.

Bactrian camel
• lives in Asia
• rocky deserts
• two humps

Bactrian and Arabian
• live in hot areas
• three eyelids per eye
• two sets of eyelashes
• can go without food or
  water for a long time

Arabian camel
• lives in Africa
• sandy deserts
• one hump

19 **Read and write.**

1. Do camels live in cold places?

_____

2. How many humps do Bactrian camels have?

_____

3. Where do Arabian camels live?

_____

4. Can camels close up their noses when it is windy?

_____

20 **Choose an animal.** Describe it. What can it do? Write.

big	claws	climb
colorful	ears	fly
long	feathers	hop
sharp	legs	jump
short	tail	run
small	teeth	swim
strong	trunk	swing

_____

_____

_____

_____

_____

21 **Write an animal poem.**

In the park with my _____.

I see a little _____.

I look up in the _____.

A _____ flies by.

22 **Find the animals.** Color and write.

I see eight animals. They are _____

_____.

23 **Read and write.** Make true sentences.

1. A monkey can _____, and I can

_____, too.

2. A parrot can _____, but I

_____.

3. A kangaroo _____.

Unit 8

The World of Work

1 **Look and write.**

2 **Work with a partner.**
Ask and answer.

a chef   a dentist
a doctor   a farmer
a firefighter   a nurse
an office worker   a police officer
a scientist   a singer
a vet

> Who's sitting at a desk?

> The office worker is sitting at a desk.

_____   _____   _____

_____   _____

_____   _____   _____

_____   _____   _____

3 **Listen to the song.** Write numbers. TR: 50

☐ I want to be a chef!

☐ I want to be a dentist!

1 I want to be a doctor!

☐ I want to be a farmer!

☐ I want to be a rock star!

☐ I want to be a singer!

4 **Write new verses for the song!** Use words from the box.

aunt	a bus driver
cousin	a firefighter
grandfather	a nurse
grandmother	an office worker
sister	a police officer
uncle	a scientist
	a vet

What does your _____ do?

He's _____. He's _____.

He's _____. Yes, he is!

What does your _____ do?

She's _____. She's _____.

She's _____. Yes, she is!

GRAMMAR

What **does** your sister **do**?	She's a vet.
What **does** his uncle **do**?	He's a firefighter.
What **do** your parents **do**?	They're office workers.
Where **do** your parents **work**?	They **work** in an office.
Where **does** her brother **work**?	He **works** on a farm.
Where **does** your sister **work**?	She **works** in an animal hospital.

5 **Read.** Look at the pictures. Write.

1. What ___does___ your cousin ___do___? She's a ___doctor___.

2. What _____ your grandpa _____? He's a _____.

3. What _____ your grandma _____? She's a _____.

4. What _____ your aunt _____? She's a _____.

5. What _____ your brother _____? He's a _____.

6 **Listen and write.** TR: 51

1. She _____ in a hospital.   4. He _____ at home.

2. He _____ in a school.   5. He _____ on a train.

3. She _____ in an office.   6. She _____ on a farm.

7 **Listen.** Read. Write questions. Underline answers. TR: 52

1. What _____ her father _____? He's **a scientist / a chef**.

2. Where _____ her mom work? She works **in a kitchen /
   at home**.

3. What _____ her aunt and uncle _____? They're
   firefighters / farmers.

4. What _____ her brother _____? He's **a bus driver /
   an office worker**.

5. Where _____ her brother work? He works **on a bus /
   in an office**.

8 **Read and write.**

My Family's Work by Amy

My father is a scientist, and my mother is a vet. My brother is an
office worker, and my sister is a doctor. I want to be a police officer.

1. What _____ Amy's father _____? _____ a scientist.

2. What _____ Amy's brother _____? _____ an office
   worker.

3. What _____ Amy's sister _____? _____ a doctor.

9 **Read and match.** Draw lines.

1. Who sings to people?   a. a soccer player
2. Who plays soccer?   b. an artist
3. Who is in the movies?   c. an inventor
4. Who makes new things?   d. a rock star
5. Who draws and paints pictures?   e. a movie star

10 **Unscramble the words.** Write.

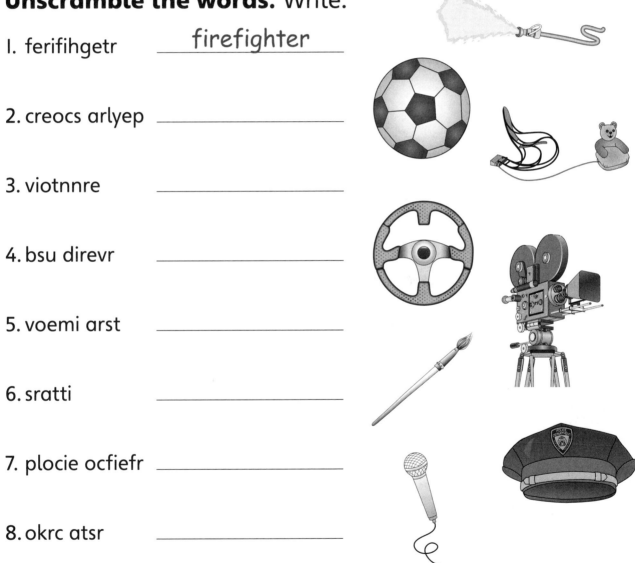

1. ferifihgetr   _firefighter_

2. creocs arlyep _____

3. viotnnre   _____

4. bsu direvr   _____

5. voemi arst   _____

6. sratti   _____

7. plocie ocfiefr _____

8. okrc atsr   _____

11 **Work with a partner.** Student I, go to page 125.
Student 2, go to page 126. Take turns.

12 **Listen and write.** TR: 53

1. What _____ your brother want to be?

2. He _____ an artist.

3. What do your sisters _____?

4. They _____ inventors.

5. What _____ you want to be one day?

6. I _____ a rock star.

13 **Look, read, and write.**

1. He likes clean teeth. What does he want to be?

   He _____.

2. She likes to work in the sun. What does she want to be?

   She _____.

3. She likes to play soccer. What does she want to be?

   She _____.

4. He likes school. What does he want to be?

   He _____.

14 Read and write.

1. Where does the teacher work? She _____

   _____ .

2. Where does the chef work? He _____

   _____ .

3. What does he want to be? He _____

   _____ .

4. What does she want to be? She _____

   _____ .

15 Do the puzzle. Read. Write.

1. This person works on a farm.

2. This person works in a hospital.

3. This person works with animals.

4. This person works with teeth.

5. This person works in a kitchen.

6. This person works in a hospital, too.

7. This person draws and paints pictures.

8. This person works in a school.

9. This person sings.

10. What does this person do? This person is a _____ .

16 Listen and read. Can you say these fast? TR: 54

1. My father's a firefighter.

2. Sister Susie sings seven songs.

3. The bus driver drives a big bus.

Listen and read. TR: 55

The Dog Whisperer

Cesar Millan helps dogs. Some dogs have problems. They are worried or scared. Some dogs bite. People call Cesar Millan the "Dog Whisperer" because he teaches bad dogs how to be good.

Cesar knows what dogs like and need. Dogs need a leader. They need to have rules. Cesar teaches dogs that he is their leader. Cesar teaches dog owners how to be their dog's leader.

Cesar walks and runs with dogs because dogs need exercise. Cesar likes to run in the mountains with dogs. He can run for four hours with a big group of dogs!

The dog is Cesar's favorite animal. Cesar loves his job because he is always working with dogs.

Dogs can learn more than a hundred words. Some dogs understand as many words as a young child understands!

18 **Read.** Check **T** for *True* and **F** for *False*.

1. Cesar Millan helps dogs. ⓉⒻ
2. Dogs need to run in the mountains. ⓉⒻ
3. Cesar's favorite animal is the frog. ⓉⒻ
4. Cesar loves his job. ⓉⒻ

19 **Look and read.** Write.

What does Cesar teach dogs?

• He teaches _____ dogs to be _____.

What problems do dogs have?

• They are worried or scared.

• _____

Cesar Millan
Job: helps dogs

What do dogs like and need?

• They need a leader.
• They need rules.

• _____

What does Cesar teach people who have dogs?

• _____

20 **Work with a partner.** Read. Write ✓ for *yes*. Write ✗ for *no*. Compare answers. Talk about jobs you want one day.

	you	your partner
Do you want a job like Cesar's?		
Do you want to help animals?		
Do you want to help people?		

21 **Choose a job.** Describe it. Who does it? Where do they work? What do they wear? What do they do? Write. Use some words from the box.

at a desk	dress	brush
at home	gloves	clean
in an office	hat	draw
inside	jacket	paint
on TV	pants	run
outside	shoes	talk

_____

_____

_____

_____

22 **Write a poem about work.** Look at the picture.

What do _____ do?

They can _____.

They work in a _____.

Come and look!

23 Read, look, and write.

1. What does she do?

   She's _____.

   Where does she work?

   She _____ in a hospital.

2. What does he do?

   He's _____.

   Where does he work?

   He _____ in a school.

3. What do they do?

   They're _____.

   Where do they work?

   They _____ in an office.

4. What does she want to

   be one day?

   She _____.

5. What does he want to

   be one day?

   He _____.

24 What about you? Write. Compare your answer with a partner's. Are they the same?

What do you want to be one day? I _____.

Unit 9

Let's Eat!

1 Look and write.

_____

_____

_____

_____

_____

_____

_____   _____   _____

_____   _____   _____

2 **Work with a partner.** Ask and answer.

> Do you eat ice cream in the morning?

> No, I eat ice cream in the afternoon and evening.

3 **Listen to the song.** Write. Draw lines to match. TR: 56

Let's eat!
Do you like _____?

Let's eat!
Do you like _____?

Let's eat!
Are there any _____?

Let's eat!
Is there any _____?

Are there any _____?

Is there any _____?
May I have some, please?

4 **Write another verse for the song!** Use some words from the box.

corn	peppers	tomato	salad
noodles	potatoes	pizza	sandwich

I like _____.

And you like _____.

Let's make a _____!

Are there **any** carrots? No, there aren't **any** carrots.

Are there **any** beans? Yes, there are.

Are there **any** peppers and mangoes? Yes, there are.

Is there **any** pasta? No, there isn't **any** pasta.

Is there **any** meat? Yes, there is.

5 **Listen.** Read and circle. TR: 57

1. No, there aren't any noodles.   Yes, there are.

2. No, there isn't any corn.   Yes, there is.

3. No, there isn't any ice cream.   Yes, there is.

4. No, there aren't any potatoes.   Yes, there are.

5. No, there aren't any tomatoes.   Yes, there are.

6 **Read.** Write the foods in the correct columns in the chart.

bread
corn
eggs
fish
hamburgers
ice cream
mangoes
potatoes

Is there any. . . ?	Are there any. . . ?
bread	

7 **Work with a partner.** Student 1, go to page 125. Student 2, go to page 126. Take turns.

8 **Look at the picture.** Read and write.

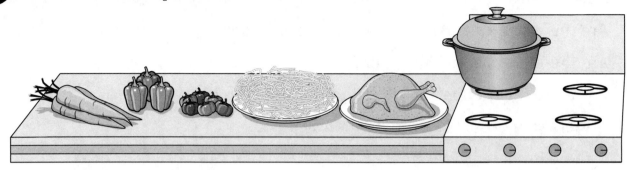

1. Are there __any__ beans?

   No, there aren't any beans.

2. Is there __any__ pasta?

   Yes, there is.

3. Are there _____ tomatoes?

   _____

4. Are there _____ eggs?

   _____

5. Is there _____ chicken?

   _____

6. Are there _____ carrots?

   _____

7. Is there _____ corn?

   _____

9 **Look and write.** Use words from the box.

cheese   chips   grapes   nuts   snacks   yogurt

_____

_____

_____

_____

_____

_____

10 **Work with a partner.** What snacks do you like?
Ask and answer. Read and check ✓.

Do you like cheese as a snack?

Yes, I like cheese.

Snacks	You like	You don't like	Your partner likes	Your partner doesn't like
carrots				
cheese				
chips				
grapes				
ice cream				
mangoes				
nuts				
yogurt				

11 **Write questions.** Write the words in the correct order.

1. have / cheese, / I / please / May / some / ?

   _____

2. some / we / May / milk, / have / please / ?

   _____

3. ice cream, / we / please / have / May / some / ?

   _____

4. I / have / carrots, / May / some / please / ?

   _____

5. we / pasta, / have / please / some / May / ?

   _____

12 **Listen and write.** TR: 58

1. _____ I have some nuts, please? Yes. Sure.

2. _____ we have some bread, please? Not right now.

3. _____ we have some cheese, please? Yes, here you are.

4. _____ I have a snack, please? Not right now. Dinner is at eight.

13 Play a game. Start at A. Listen and draw a line. TR: 59

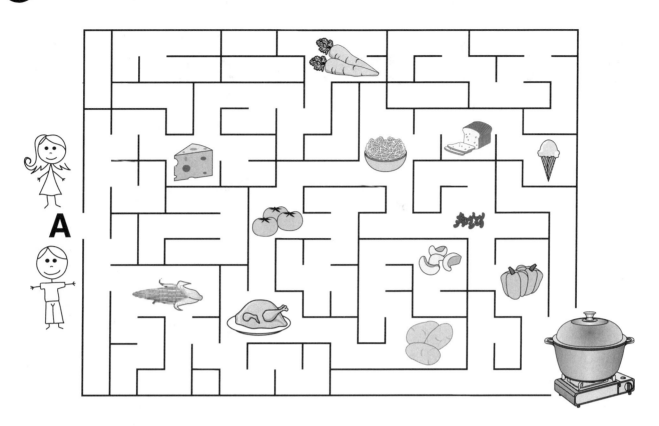

14 Look at Activity 13. What foods are there? Write.

I see _____

_____

_____

_____ .

15 Listen and read. Can you say these fast? TR: 60

1. Lucy likes peppers on her pizza.

2. Charlie's eating cheese with his chips.

3. May we have tomatoes, potatoes, noodles, and nuts?

Super Foods!

Some foods help you grow and learn. They help people be healthy, too. They are super foods! Do you know what foods are good for you?

Chicken, meat, fish, beans, eggs, and nuts are good for you. Brown rice and whole grains are good for you, too.

Milk and foods made from milk are good for you. Cheese and yogurt are made from milk. These foods make your bones strong. Fish and many kinds of vegetables make your bones strong, too.

Fruits and vegetables are great foods! There are fruits and vegetables of many colors. Eat a few different colors every day! You can eat a red tomato, a yellow banana, purple grapes, green peppers, and orange carrots. Eat some leafy green vegetables, too.

Some plants eat meat. They eat insects, frogs, and birds!

Candy and sugary foods taste good, but don't eat too much of them. Instead, eat super foods most of the time! They can keep you strong and healthy.

17 **Read.** Check **T** for *True* and **F** for *False*.

1. Fish and nuts are good for you.   (T) (F)
2. Cheese and yogurt make your bones strong.   (T) (F)
3. Fruits and vegetables aren't good for you.   (T) (F)
4. Eat candy and sugary foods most of the time.   (T) (F)

18 **Read and check.**

	Good for you	Makes bones strong	Don't eat too much
cheese	✓	✓	
chicken			
fish			
milk			
candy			
sugary foods			
fruit			
vegetables			

19 **Work with a partner.** What super foods do you eat?
Ask and answer. Write.

I eat fish. Do you eat fish?

I do. I eat nuts, too. Do you eat nuts?

	Me	My partner
Super foods		

20 **What is your favorite dinner?** When do you eat it? What do you drink with it? How does it taste? Write. Use some words from the box.

| beans | carrots | cheese | chicken | corn |
| fish | noodles | rice | peppers | tomatoes |

My favorite dinner is _____

_____

_____

_____.

21 **Draw and write.** Draw a picture of a breakfast you like to eat. Write about the foods at your breakfast. How does your breakfast taste?

I like to eat _____

_____.

My breakfast tastes _____.

114

22 (Circle) the foods. Answer the questions. Write.

1. Are there any peppers? <u>No, there aren't any peppers.</u>

2. Is there any ice cream? _____

3. Are there any hamburgers? _____

4. Are there any potatoes? _____

5. Is there any salad? _____

6. What foods are there? _____

_____

23 **Look at the picture.** What is the girl asking her mom? Write.

_____ I have some _____, please?

Review

1 **Read, look, and write.**

I. What does she do?

She's _____.

2. What does he do?

He's _____.

3. What does she do?

She's _____.

Where does she work?

She _____ outside.

2 **Listen and write.** TR: 62

I. What _____ you _____ one day?

2. I _____ a chef.

3. _____ I have some nuts, please?

4. _____ we have some snacks, please?

3 **Read and write.** Use words from the box. Draw lines to match.

can   can't   do   does   doesn't   don't

1. Can a parrot fly?

    Yes, it _____.

2. Do giraffes have long necks?

    Yes, they _____.

3. Can crocodiles hop?

    No, they _____.

4. Does a tiger have colorful feathers?

    No, it _____.

5. Do penguins swing?

    No, they _____.

4 **Look at the picture.** Read and answer.

1. Are there any carrots? _____

2. Are there any peppers? _____

3. Is there any corn? _____

4. Is there any bread? _____

Unit 1   Student I Use with Activity I2 on page 9.

12 **Listen.** Look. Circle.

Tell about the pictures. Check your partner's answers.

Unit 2   Student I Use with Activity I6 on page 23.

16 **Work with a partner.** Look at the chart. Pick a day of the week.

1. Ask, "What's the weather like?"

2. Listen to your partner's answer.

3. Tell your partner what to wear.

4. Take turns.

Unit 3   Student I Use with Activity 20 on page 35.

20 **Work with a partner.** Look and read. Ask. Draw.

1. Look at the chart. Ask your partner what the boy and girl like to do.
2. Listen to your partner's answer. Draw 😊 for *yes*. Draw 😐 for *no*.

Do they like to play tag?

Yes, they like to play tag.

Do they like to play soccer?

No, it's boring.

| play tag | play soccer | watch a game | skateboard | fly a kite | throw a ball |

Unit 4   Student I Use with Activity 18 on page 49.

18 **Tell about the picture.** Then check your partner's answer.

Listen. Look. Circle.

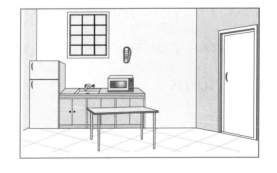

Unit 1   Student 2 Use with Activity 12 on page 9.

12 **Tell about the pictures.** Check your partner's answers.

Listen. Look. Circle.

Unit 2   Student 2 Use with Activity 16 on page 23.

16 **Work with a partner.** Look at the chart. Pick a day of the week.

1. Ask, "What's the weather like?"

2. Listen to your partner's answer.

3. Tell your partner what to wear.

4. Take turns.

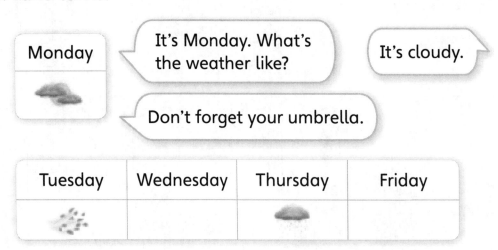

Tuesday	Wednesday	Thursday	Friday

20 **Work with a partner.** Look and read. Ask. Draw.

1. Look at the chart. Ask your partner what the boy and girl like to do.

2. Listen to your partner's answer. Draw 😊 for *yes*. Draw 😐 for *no*.

| play tag | play soccer | watch a game | skateboard | fly a kite | throw a ball |

Unit 5   Student I Use with Activity 10 on page 58.

10 **Work with a partner.**
Tell about the pictures.
Ask, "What time is it?"
Listen and write
the answers.

Look at the pictures.
Answer your partner's
questions. Check your
partner's answers.

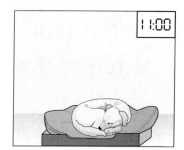

Unit 4 Student 2 Use with Activity 18 on page 49.

18 **Listen.** Look. Circle.

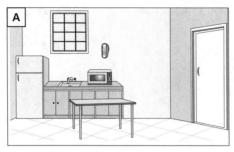 

Tell about the picture.
Then check your partner's
answer.

Unit 5 Student 2 Use with Activity 10 on page 58.

10 **Work with a partner.**
Look at the pictures.
Answer your partner's
questions. Check your
partner's answers.

**Tell about the
pictures.** Ask,
"What time is it?"
Listen and write the
answers.

 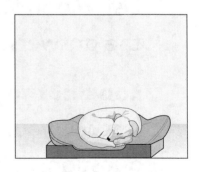

12 **Listen.** Look. Circle.

  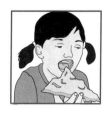  

Tell about the pictures. Check your partner's answers.

Unit 7   Student I Use with Activity I4 on page 87.

14 **Your partner has a photo of one of these animals.**
   Ask questions to your partner. Check your partner's animal.

Does your animal have a long tail?   No, it doesn't.

Can your animal fly?   No, it can't.

Answer your partner's questions about your animal.

12 **Tell about the pictures.** Check your partner's answers.

Listen. Look. Circle.

14 **Answer your partner's questions about your animal.**

Does your animal have a long tail? No, he doesn't.

Can your animal fly? No, it can't.

Your partner has a photo of one of these animals.
Ask questions to your partner. Check your partner's animal.

11 **Look at the chart.** Ask about the person's work.
Listen to your partner's answers. Write.

> What does Angela do?   She's a rock star.

Angela	Lara	Paulo	Bruno
She's a rock star .	She's a _____ .	He's a _____ .	He's a _____ .

Look at the chart. Answer your partner's questions.
Check your partner's work.

Roberto	Beatriz	Bianca	Luiz

7 **Work with a partner.** Take turns asking and answering.
Write ✓ for *yes*. Write ✗ for *no*.

> Is there any chicken?   No, there isn't any chicken.

Ask your partner:		Answer your partner's questions. ✓ = yes ✗ = no	
Is there any . . . ?	**Are there any . . . ?**		
✗ chicken	☐ carrots	✓ pasta	✗ bananas
☐ ice cream	☐ mangoes	✗ rice	✗ cookies
☐ meat	☐ noodles	✓ milk	✓ hamburgers
☐ tea	☐ oranges	✓ salad	✓ peppers

11 **Look at the chart.** Answer your partner's questions. Check your partner's work.

What does Angela do?   She's a rock star.

Angela	Lara	Paulo	Bruno

Look at the chart. Answer your partner's questions. Check your partner's work.

Roberto	Beatriz	Bianca	Luiz
He's a chef .	She's a _____ .	She's a _____ .	He's an _____ .

Unit 9   Student 2 Use with Activity 7 on page 107.

7 **Work with a partner.** Take turns asking and answering. Write ✓ for *yes*. Write ✗ for *no*.

Is there any chicken?   No, there isn't any chicken.

Ask your partner:		Answer your partner's questions. ✓ = yes ✗ = no	
Is there any. . . ?	Are there any. . . ?		
☐ pasta	☐ bananas	✗ chicken	✗ carrots
☐ rice	☐ cookies	✗ ice cream	✓ mangoes
☐ milk	☐ hamburgers	✗ meat	✓ noodles
☐ salad	☐ peppers	✓ tea	✗ oranges